Corrected

Convicted

Accepted

Corrected

Convicted

Accepted

The Journey Which Began Is The Journey Which Remains

Apostle Joseph Paul Brown

authorHOUSE®

AuthorHouse™ LLC
1663 Liberty Drive
Bloomington, IN 47403
www.authorhouse.com
Phone: 1-800-839-8640

Published by AuthorHouse 07/10/2014

ISBN: 978-1-4969-2635-7 (sc)
ISBN: 978-1-4969-2634-0 (e)

Library of Congress Control Number: 2014912442

ABOUT THE AUTHOR

Apostle Joseph Paul Brown is the founder and Pastor of The Miracle Temple of Prophetic Outreach Church. He is the Chief Apostle of The Prophetic Outreach Movement in fellowship with other churches, as well as planting new churches. Joseph Paul Brown is the founder of the Prophetic Outreach Radio Broadcast and the host of Prophetic Insight Television spreading the word on line. Looking forward to further the TV program to a broader network of television channels in the future. The Apostle is gifted in many areas and utilizes his gifts and abilities for Christ and the work of the Lord. He also promotes education and inspires the youth to strive for excellence in learning. He earnestly desires that all young people will push towards their future and hold fast to the faith while pursuing their goals, enduring any tasks that comes with obstacles and adversity. Education brought through life's lessons, as learned by the author, you will find that he uses it as a tool to lead, to build lives, and to win souls for Christ. This has proven to be successful in the efforts of his ministry. His purpose for this book has expanded in the like same manner which he foresees the impact of his testimony to reach those who are imprisoned spiritually, mentally, emotionally, and or physically.

TABLE OF CONTENTS

ACKNOWLEDGEMENTS

I would like to take this opportunity to make mention of a few people that allowed God to use them inspirationally in my life and ministry throughout all of the ups and downs. **THANKS!** *(To all of you.)*

To Bishop C.L. Bryant: Thanks for your leadership and teaching along the way.

To the Late Pastor W.G. Richards: I grew up under his leadership, was mentored at the final chapter of his life, and nursed back to good spiritual health at his message. Praise God.

To Dr. J.L. Johnson: Who always had a word of comfort and encouragement. He always knew what to say. Great Man of God, I thank you!

To my mother, Ms. Frankie Jackson: *My Lord*! A woman who will not give up on her children. God bless you mother. I love you!

To my Grandmother: *My God!* The late Mother Ruth Masters. I will see you when I get to heaven!!!

To my whole family: You know it's too many of us to name everyone. Much love to all of you.

To my dad, Rickey Brown Sr.: Thanks for all of your words along the way.

To my Grandmother: *My God!* The one and only, Pastor Ann Lang. Thanks for all that you do.

There are so many people that I would love to name in my acknowledgements. Let me openly say that whatever you did or said that worked for me: Thank You!!!!

Last, but will never be the least, to my very own Apostle, Pastor Richard Jose. He opened the doors of ministry to me and remains as a mentor to me. Thanks.

PREFACE

Young Man's Journey

The steps of a good man are ordered by the Lord. What a great deal of comfort and satisfaction it is to know and have the benefit of an all knowing and all caring Father. One who searches the heart of man; observing his afflictions and examining his meditations.

In my life's journey, I have pursued lots of ideas in the quest to find success. I've made several mistakes and encountered a countless number of disappointments. I, therefore, found it difficult to maintain a positive perspective withstanding such unfortunate events.

A young man's dream, a young man's passion, all seemed to have been swallowed up from a distance. Derailed by worldly opposition, spiritually weakened, and *fleshly* driven, yet still reminded of my true identity.

So thankful for the voice that I heard: *"You know who you are and you know who you belong to. You do not have to face your circumstances alone. Come back to me. Receive my council and be healed. I, The Lord, shall make your life purposeful and meaningful."*

Yes, it would be to a young man's advantage to have received such a word of encouragement during his time of isolation, suffering, and despair……As a wounded son searches for aid, lifts his eyes, and falls to his knees, surprisingly, but undoubtedly he receives an answer. A discovery has been made which so rightfully deserves acceptance, followed by the right response!

A change had to be made. A change was needed that would redirect my focus and enlighten my understanding within this period of difficulty; Replacing my current thoughts of failure with thoughts of security, discipline, and correction. Motivations of respect and appreciation for God's character and His will to straighten the pathway of my feet.

With humility and cheer, it has been one of my greatest desires to release and share this life and mind changing experience, a testimony of my life. How bitterness, sorrow, anger, rebellion, brokenness, deprivation, discomfort, lack of resources, mental distress, emotional disturbances, shame, humiliation, and a struggle within myself led to misery and feelings of being less than a man. How all of this turned to triumph, victory, peace, and happiness. How an overload of burdens can be lifted and how relief from guilt is admitted. Transformed from a low-life mentality to a humble and better self-applied view of who I am, what I could be, and how far I could go in this life and in the life to come.

[All found in scripture, inspired and gained as I kneel before God in prayer.......]

May whoever reads this testimony of my life, and the solutions provided by the Word, be eternally blessed and healed in the name of our Lord and Savior, Jesus Christ. Amen!

SCRIPTURE OPENING

Proverbs 3:11-12

My son, despise not the chastening of the Lord; Neither be weary of his correction;

For whom the Lord loveth, he correcteth even as a father the son in whom he delighteth.

Proverbs 13:18

Poverty and shame shall be to him that refuseth instruction; but he that regardeth reproof shall be honoured.

2 Timothy 3: 16-17

All scripture is given by inspiration of God, and is profitable for reproof, for correction, for instruction in righteousness.

That the man of God may be perfect, thoughly furnished unto all good works.

2 Timothy 4:2

Preach the word; be instant in season, out of season; reprove, rebuke, exhort with all longsuffering and doctrine.

FIGURING IT ALL OUT

CHAPTER 1

It all begins here. The discernment of a son with an attitude; distressed, unduly, burdened, pressed in with perplexity, and uncalculated issues of misery. A pilgrim at heart with a low class of self-esteem. A descriptive journey with only one hope, one answer and one solution in the midst of *this* dry valley of adversity and high mountain of affliction. In essence, the entity of being in a world of trouble.

THE CARE OF AFFLICTION

I've found that I must not despise, or get weary of it. It is heavy, long, and unbearable, but I cannot faint. Observing the biblical example of the Apostles, I am not to be dispirited, driven to despair, and I will not use indirect means to rectify grievance. Although difficult at times, I am not to think that it will grow harder and neither will it last longer than it should, because deliverance comes in certainty!

What is my comfort *out* of this entire affliction?

That hope.

That answer.

That solution.

It is, that it is, a divine correction. It is from God. Therefore, it must not be despised. I must not grow weary, for God knows both what I need and what I can bear.

Such can be seen as "fatherly" correction; which does not come from vindictive justice, but fatherly affection.

The love of a true father to rebuke me, and chasten me. (Revelation 3:19)

THRONE ROOM INSTRUCTIONS

CHAPTER 2

"Instructions from the throne room, walking in my shoes I shall not refuse!"

"Happy at the rod of correction, learning to <u>be</u> with all appreciation."

"I'm humbled enough to be instructed......."

"I refuse to let pride get me; like that no one can be taught and will certainly be abased."

"Where there is correction, there is conviction."

"Where there is conviction, there is acceptance."

"Where there is acceptance, there is a response."

-Apostle Joseph Paul Brown

An angel rebuked a prophet because of his slow response. Just the same, the angel Gabriel, rebuked Zechariah. He was rebuked for doubt and disbelief in the word that was sent from God, that his aged wife would give birth to a son, John the forerunner of Jesus. (Luke 1:5-20)

I would conclude that this example of chastisement, which would seem harsh and somewhat over the edge, was meant to correct and convict this man, so that the next time a word was sent from God, his response would be to believe it and accept it. As the story continues, we find that the angel ordered an affliction to come upon Zechariah. He was unable to speak, made to remain dumb until God's word had come to pass. After the birth of John the Baptist, Zechariah's speech was returned to him.

Some of us could be in a similar situation of *reform* as this. Examining the situation, we could be asking ourselves: "Am I where I am simply because I don't believe all of God's word? Am I failing to believe that whatever He has promised to me shall come to pass?"

Yes! I have learned a lesson in this particular reform. God will cause certain things to happen. Not necessarily to push us away, but to bring us closer to Him, that we may believe that nothing is impossible in Him.

By His word, everything is created.

By His word, anything can be destroyed.

His word is the beginning and the end.

His word never returns void.

Thank God for the scriptures. We must understand that the scriptures are *holy*. They come from God, who is *holy*. The scriptures were delivered by *holy* men. The scriptures contain *holy* commands, and were designed to make us *holy*. The scriptures will lead us to *holiness*. They are distinguished from worldly or secular writings, writing of morale, and other literary pieces that fail to promote the Kingdom of God.

Thank God for the Word. For it makes me wise to salvation, and it guides me in the way of eternal life. It instructs us in that which is true. It corrects us when we are faulty, and directs in that which is right.

Thank God for the Word. For it is profitable in all areas of the Christian life; for correction, for instruction in righteousness, for conviction which proceeds.......

I've been corrected.

I am convicted.

It is accepted.

THE OPERATION OF THE FLESH

CHAPTER 3

The operation of the flesh will never cooperate with any spiritual guidance, council, rebuke, reformation, or correction. Even when it is convicted, it is left behind, unaccepted, unappreciated, and often times mocked within rejection.

This is truth with believers and non-believers. A non-believer is of the flesh, which makes him all about *flesh*. A believer can operate in the flesh, which in turn makes him receptive to the things of the *flesh*. By this he is weakened and has an inability to respond spiritually to practical truths and corrections that are given to emancipate his *fleshly* walk. Either way, flesh is *flesh*.

Whether in the life of a believer or non-believer, all *flesh* wars against the spirit. The *flesh* will not obey a spiritual command. If we obey the flesh, then we disobey the spirit. This makes us a *believer* and not a follower. We believe, but fail to follow. At this point, we are following in after the flesh, and not the spirit. Therefore, we are controlled by the flesh and not by the spirit. Being controlled by the flesh, and not the spirit, warps our mind into carnality. Having a carnal mind is death. A carnal mind is enmity against God. It will not obey God's law.

God wants to correct us, bringing us into submission to His will and way.

"I am a witness."

Believing in God does not make us right with God. Obeying God's word makes us right with him. Out of an act of love, God will do everything that He can do to chastise and correct us before it is too late. (Romans 8:1-7)

In the beginning of my teens, I walked with God, at the age of thirteen to be exact. As I began to age, I began to become somewhat acquainted with the things of the flesh, rather than the things of the spirit. The Bible refers to those that slip away from things of the spirit, as "backsliders". Some people would say, "Oh! That normally happens to a lot us." Others would say, "You were just young and not sure of yourself." Another group would say, "You're not perfect. Everybody makes mistakes."............

Yes! Each of these responses has a form of truth, but if we're not careful, it can be deceptive, thus becoming a crutch to keep us from ever being consistent in a spiritual walk. It will become a mouth, full of excuses. Such could imply that what we do is pardoned as a result of a *fleshly* nature, indicating that it is impossible to live a spiritual life that is separated from sin and *flesh.*

This explains the war pattern that that flesh has against the spirit, and that the spirit has against the *flesh.*

During the time of my "backslidden" state, I never made any excuses for what I was doing, but others made excuses for me; which I never accepted, knowing the truth for myself. Sin has a grip on so many people, and in return they make more and more excuses to keep doing it. As a backslider, sin had a grip on my life. After suffering the consequences of the habits that I created in sin, I found it easy to get <u>in</u> a hard to get <u>out</u>. I found it easy to start, and hard to stop. I could name a lot of sin that was in my life. Just as much as anyone else can name sin that was previously or is currently in their life. On the contrary, it really doesn't matter at this point.

I had to relocate, and *find* Jesus all over again. I needed His power to deliver me from every habit that I had developed, and most of all, from the spirit that was driving me to do it.

In every sin that is hard to stop, there is an evil spirit that is behind it.

In order to break the cycle of habitual sin, the spirit of that sin must be dealt with. We can never get rid of the spirit of that sin unless we first get rid of the excuses that we have made for it. Meaning, we have to want to be changed.

We can observe the flesh and look at the many responses that it has to offer. Especially when it comes to correction and conviction.

1.   A person of the *flesh* has a negative attitude.

<u>Example</u>:

"I'm not going to quit until I get ready."
"I'm grown. I do what I want to."

Others with similar attitudes of rebellion hold to their ignorance and live as if they can escape the fate of total and eternal damnation in hell.

<u>Note</u>:

We don't have any control over rather we live or die. Nor do we know when our time will come. That's why we are to live our lives, not in rebellion, but in the obedience of God's will. Seeking to understand and learn how to live *right*.

2.   A person of the *flesh* does not care.

  <u>Example</u>:

  "I'm set in my ways."
  "I've been this way all of my life."
  "I don't care about you, me, or nobody else."

Others with similar attitudes are bound by depression and have given up on any possibility of change. A spirit of confusion controls this particular type of mind, where nothing matters and neither life, nor *death* itself, has any value to them.

<u>Note</u>:

We can find the spirit of these same attitudes not just in the streets, but also in the church. There are some people who can sit and listen to a soul-winning message, preached with power, correction, and conviction, and allow these same spirits to rob them of the opportunity to receive Jesus and the truth of the gospel.

3.   A person of the *flesh* is satisfied.

  <u>Example</u>:

> *"I do what I do because it feels good."*
> *"I can't live without it."*
> *"Let me do my thing and you do yours."*

Others with similar attitudes are "self-righteous", holding to their own belief system, living by the concepts of societal liberty, where every man is entitled to believe as he pleases.

Note:

Satan has used that and these things, which man's laws permits, to deceive the hearts and minds of many. This too is a rebellion in ignorance. For no matter what you say, people like this have not the heart *for* change. For them, change is not an option. Free-will is mistaken and God's grace is taken for granted, as if God accepts *any* way of living.

We hear people say:

"Just repent and live how you please." (This way of thinking is FALSE)

"God requires a standard way of living known as holiness." (By faith we can live in holiness)

What about mistakes? We must repent and turn from them.

"Yes. We *might* make mistakes, but we do not live to make them." – Bishop C.L. Bryant.

Yes. We have a continuous war going on between the flesh, against the spirit. This is the most outrageous and relentless battle ever fought. Here we have two different natures: A *divine nature* and a *sinful nature*. The flesh is contrary to the spirit. It cannot please God.

Both natures have their own desires. One desires evil and the other desires holiness. This always has been and always will be an eternal conflict, offering an eternal fate. Choose eternal life or eternal death. Heaven or hell.

The wages of sin is death, but the gift of God is eternal life through Jesus Christ our Lord. (Romans 6:23)

If any man be in Christ, he is a new creation: Old things are passed away; Behold all things become new. (2 Corinthians 5:17)

The flesh only pleases the flesh. It only takes pleasure in doing everything opposite of how the spirit would have us to do.

What do we see in the flesh?
What do we feel in the flesh?
How do we respond in the flesh?

What do we see in the spirit?
What do we feel in the spirit?
How do we respond in the spirit?

Both, living in the flesh and living in the spirit, provide a way of living here in the world. One is right, one is wrong. One is perverted, one is pure. One is evil, one is holy. One offers life, one offers death. We are given free-will to choose who we will serve.

The original plan for sex was that it would be a gift to married couples. (Man and Woman.) It can be perverted by the flesh!

Having sex before marriage is opposite of God's ordination for its use. In our day and time, sex is used as one of the greatest abominations and rebellions. It is sold, prostituted, and advertised. Perversion has warped man's mind. Our women are raped, our children are molested, and homosexuals are out of control.

(God made man for woman, and woman for man. Get Married!)

As I could go on with this topic, dealing with the operations of the flesh, I would rather move on to the next.........

Let me not overload you with information that you already know, and that makes perfect sense.

CORRECTED
CONVICTED
ACCEPTED

CHAPTER 4

I grew up in a single parent home, consisting of my mother and other family members. I was not a problem child, but there were still some things that I had to learn on my own. One of the most important things that I had to learn, really slow, was how to listen. My uncle, the Late-Pastor W.G. Richards, always said "You have two ears and one mouth. That means that you listen more than you talk."

A lot of us in this generation don't want to hear what people have to say. Some of the mistakes that I made were simply because I did not listen. I did what I wanted to do. As a result, I had to pay for each of the mistakes that I made.

Sad to say, but in life today, I've seen people suffering the consequences of their bad choices. Paying the penalty, and in response; instead of correcting the mistakes that they made, they make others pay for them in their stead. Thus bringing hardship on others....They would rather take their frustration out on peers and even loved ones. (Hum! Interesting.)

Note:

Failing to hold ourselves responsible for our own actions, will never solve anything.

In my failures, mistakes, and bad choices I was always the first to admit that I was wrong. (No matter what.) "It's me oh Lord, standing in the need of prayer."

Even when I could not get it together, I acknowledged and confessed my faults. For this reason, I never really needed anyone else to beat me over the head, telling me that I was wrong. Nevertheless, I would receive it anyway.

If we cannot confess where we are wrong, accepting it as so, then we surely will not be able to accept and appreciate anyone else saying anything to us. It is definitely a natural affection to want to hear something that sounds good, and that hypes the sensors of our emotions. Thus making us feel good. But, what about *that* which makes us feel bad for good?

13

Well, Proverbs 27:5-6 says,

"Open rebuke is better than secret love."

"Faithful are the wounds of a friend; but the kisses of an enemy are deceitful."

So, we find that unconcealed love will administer reproofs that are needed. We find that a true friend will correct you and the wounds will heal, but your enemy will tell you what sounds good, deceitfully, which will never offer the healing that you are in need of.

My God! "What a waste." We spend all of this time in error, listening to what we want to listen to. We take in all this hype, only to find that the road that we have been traveling on is just some high-hoped and fleshly-driven idea that leads to destruction, both physically and emotionally. And just to top it off, we have somehow set ourselves up for spiritual destruction as well.

Don't!! Tell!! Me!! I Sound Good!!! When I sing, and sound like Wes Craven's worst nightmare!!!

As most would say, "I was only trying to encourage you".

NO! NO! This is no different from telling a lie. It would encourage me more if you told me to go (somewhere) and practice. Or perhaps you could encourage me to invest in vocal coaching lessons, that will teach me how to sing; seeing that singing is where my heart is.

To make me feel as though I am doing a good job at something that I am not, is deceitful. It is a set-up for public embarrassment. This kind of wound will take quite some time to heal; If it heals at all, depending upon what type or color it is.

What do you mean *color*, preacher? Lol!!!

Proverbs 20:30 says,

The blueness of a wound cleanseth away evil: so do stripes the inward parts of the belly.

Blue: If you take the suffix –ness from the word blueness, you have a color. Combining them together, you have some sort of color, the same color explaining its color.

As to how it got there, the purpose of it being there, and the results of it being there:

The blueness occurred from a blow, a strike, or a swing if you would. The purpose of the blow, examining its color, was to cleanse away evil, more so to correct. Its stripes or strokes (if you would), reaching the innermost parts, suggests that healing is the result. For healing always begins from within before working its way out.

Are there any other colors?

I would say so. For bruises always have a way of changing colors.

A bruise can start off red. Then it changes to blue, then to purple, and then to black.

So, when I say, "What type of color it is", I am not referring to different colors, but I am referring to the type of wound that it is.

The wounds from a foolish enemy were meant to cause error and provide harm. The wound from a wise friend was meant to cause correction and provide healing.

Overtime, I learned not to let "just anybody" mentor me. I got so good at it that when they thought I was listening, I wasn't. And when they did not think that I was listening, I was….. Lol!!! Sounds crazy doesn't it? Let me explain more.

I had to develop a type of spiritual discernment that would help me determine if whether the information that was being transmitted was for my good, or for my bad. What? Yes!!!

Backing up to <u>Proverbs 20:29</u>:

The glory of young men is their strength; and the beauty of old men is the grey head.

This suggests that young men can bend, but will not break. The grey hair of old men refers to experience and wisdom.

Now, over the course of several years, I have discovered that there's no fool like and old fool….BANG!!!

OLD MEN, YOU DON'T HAVE TO LIKE ME IF THIS IS YOU.

I have been in the company of so many old, and foolish, people that are so-called, trying to "hip me to wisdom", when they did not have any wisdom themselves. They would *guarantee* me success if I took their advice, while injecting a reason as to why I should.

They would say, "Young man. You a young man. See, I been around for a L….O….N….G time, If you listen to me, you will get somewhere." Please don't take any offense to this, but *"they ain't said nothing!!!"*

I went somewhere, alright; Somewhere else. What some would call A.D.D.; I called "getting out of town in my head". It took practice, although, to know who to listen to and who not to listen to. [No disrespect.]

That's that *young men's strength.*

Okay, enough of all of this laughter.

Well, if you're not laughing by now, it's probably because you haven't heard some of the things that I've heard. Or maybe….Hum!

Moving on.

FALLING DOWN

CHAPTER 5

I never thought that falling down could be so *easy*, that getting back up could be so *hard*. Considering how long it takes for an elderly person to get up after suffering a fall, it's difficult for a young man to see himself in such a view, as we are young at the moment. After all, if I fall, I'll just spring back up, and that's that.

Well, let's look at a spiritual and corrupted fall in comparison to the physical fall of an elderly person.

When comparing the two, we find that there is no difference except, falling down spiritually and being corrupted has nothing to do with age. Regardless of how old or young a person is, in this case, a fall is just a fall. Biblically, this kind of fall is just as hard to get back up from, as it is for an elderly person to get back up from a physical fall….if not harder.

The song, "We fall down, but we get up…." (Donnie McClurkin) is a very nice song. On the contrary, some of you would not agree with me when I say that this song makes it sound pretty easy to just get back up again. Yet, it is not that easy.

Even the word of the Lord declares that once one has been cleansed from a demon, that same devil will come right back, and if there is no spiritual growth or in-filling, it comes back in with seven more demons, making that person's spiritual health worse off than it was before.

Falling down is very dangerous. We as Christians should practice planting our feet in a way so that we cannot, nor will not, fall under any circumstances. We all must get to this point. No other options.

We are not designed to fall. Falling is bad. Let me say that again……
Falling is bad, and true saints don't fall.

The second to the last book of the Bible, the book of Jude, ends with these words:

<u>Jude 24-25</u>:

Now unto him that is able to keep you from <u>falling</u>, and to present you faultless before the presence of his glory with exceeding joy,

To the only wise God our Savior, be glory and majesty, dominion and power, both now and forever. Amen.

On our own, we will fall, but we are not designed to fall. We are not to look forward to falling, certainly if we're serving *Him* that is able to <u>keep</u> us from <u>falling</u>.

Brother Preacher, How many times have you made mistakes?

"Several."

How many times have you fallen?

"Less than a few."

What?

That's what I said. Making mistakes is different from falling. You can make a mistake and yet remain standing, but when you fall, you are no longer standing. Big Difference! My fall was because I did not obey God, the One that is able to keep me from falling.

Yes, it is easy to fall, but hard to get back up. If this is not so, then why would we need God to <u>keep</u> us from falling?

I had to change the way that I thought about a lot of things. It was during the time of "getting back up" that my thoughts changed.

I can remember it just as well as I can remember my last name. Pastor W.G. Richards said to me, "Just because the situation is gone down, doesn't mean you have to stay down. You've got to pick yourself up!!!" This is when I learned that getting back up was hard, because I had to do it myself. God was not responsible for me falling, and He did not have to be the one responsible for picking me up. His job was to keep me from falling, not to pick me up when I fell.

How hard it was to get back up. It's easier to get back up with assistance, but not so much when you have to pick yourself up.

You can't even flow in the same anointing that you may have been used to flowing in, as you are getting back up.

Why? Because it's not *your* anointing, it's God's anointing. Disobedience is what caused you to fall. So, not only did you fall from grace, but you've also fallen from the anointing that you may have walked in prior to the fall. You can't walk in anything that you fall from. So, we first have to get back up and obey God. Then we can flow in the anointing again. Falling down is dangerous, and we are not to look forward to falling...

Note:

People who look forward to falling are people who are already down and don't want to get up.

IGNORING
CONVICTION

CHAPTER 6

People, who are willfully ignorant, stubborn, and hard-headed, are not the ones ignoring conviction. They don't have a conviction to ignore. Ironically, it is <u>us</u>: church-going, born-again believers that are ignoring conviction.

One who is convicted doesn't have to accept it. Sometimes we can hear a truth, and that's all that we did, was *hear* it. We have to take heed to the truth after we have heard the truth. For the word of the Lord also declares that we must hear the word and also do the word.

It's amazing: The things we do to ignore our convictions. We know better than to do a lot of the things that we do. We hear the Spirit speaking to us, calling us by our names before we do something wrong. We hear him saying, "Don't do that. Stop. Turn back around. Don't go over there." We hear this and in our hearts we are convicted, but we ignore it by shoving it to the side.

We shove our convictions to the side, wanting to fit in with the crowd. We shove our convictions to the side, all for a certain dollar amount. We shove our convictions to the side for popularity. We shove our convictions to the side hoping that people will like us. We shove our convictions to the side, just to have a good time.

My God!! Whatever we do, when we shove our convictions to the side, is what helps us ignore them. What we were hearing before the party got started, we can no longer hear until it's all over.

<u>Note</u>:

Conviction has a voice of its (His) own, and you don't have to be at church to hear it, because he's already in you.

CAN'T SLEEP AT NIGHT

CHAPTER 7

One sign that the spirit of *conviction* is at work in your life is when you lay down at night, hoping to go to sleep, and you can't. Not that anyone has said anything to you, but *that* which was *planted* in you at the church, or from someone who loves you, is trying to sprout up on the inside of you at the end of the day. After doing what you want to do all day, when it's time to go to sleep, *conviction* won't let you.

You have been active in sin all day, simply having fun at it. Yet, at the end of the day, *conviction* won't let you sleep. The Holy Ghost, who you have overridden, has you tossing and turning. The first thought is: "I just can't find the *sweet spot*." Regrettably, this is not the case.

There is a knock at the door in the "weeee" hours of the night that disturbs your rest.

Who wants visitors at bed time? (Unexpected visitors, that is…..)

The Holy Ghost will pay you a visit when you have not paid Him attention. Knocking on your *spiritual* door and calling you by name. (Now, that's a lot of racket.)

I know what it's like to physically have someone pounding on the door and shouting at the same time. Perhaps you too have experienced this. We know that this can become very annoying. Let's look at this from a scriptural view in order to see it with a spiritual perspective.

Revelation 3:20 says,

Behold I stand at the door, and knock: If any man hear my voice, and open the door, I will come in to him, and will sup with him, and he with me.

Interesting! Of course, spiritually speaking, this would refer to the very doors of our hearts. We would then conclude that this would only happen to someone who has not accepted Jesus into their hearts just yet. "Not So." (Speaking from experience) Anyone standing at the door, standing, knocking, or shouting, would mean that they are "out" not "in", but wanting to come in. Come in for what? Perhaps they want to come in to talk, to commune, or to fellowship. That would be the most likely answer.

There are times when we have someone knocking at our physical door, we don't want to open it. When we think about it, there may have been some times that we heard someone not only knocking, but yelling and shouting for us to open the door, suggesting that something is wrong or they simply are attempting to get our attention. Yet, we still do not open the door. In such a case, have we considered that maybe they know that we are inside, and simply are ignoring them the first, second, and third time...Hum! Mighty God!!!

How does this apply to someone who has already received Christ into their heart? The answer was already spoken when we heard Him say, *"Don't do that...Don't go over there...Don't say that...Put that down...Listen to me..."* Yet, we shoved Him to the side as He was speaking the first, second, and third time.

When we override the voice of the Holy Spirit, we are pushing Him to the side. When we push Him to the side, we are actually pushing him <u>out</u>. How? Because the Spirit of God on the *inside* of us was giving us a command and we simply did not want to obey. So, how is it possible for us to succeed at doing our own will, when the will of God, on the *inside*, is telling us to do something else?

At this point, He is no longer *in* but *outside*, once again, "standing on our front porch".

So, what else is there for Him to do?_____. You fill in the blank.

Oh yes!! Some of us are good at putting company out. When we want our visitors to leave, we have all kinds of signs and signals that we give them to let them know that it is time to go, especially if there is something else that we want to or have planned to do.

Such indirect behavior, does not paint the picture or idea of a respectful person. Yet, this is what we are doing when we disobey the voice of God as He speaks to us. Let me tell you, I can say this because this is what I did.

"Why can't I get any sleep?" Let me get up out of this bed, open the door, and find out. (This was me) The same person that I put

25

outside was the same person standing there, knocking, and calling my name.

"He wants me to pray, but I'm too lazy to get up in the middle of the night." (He's knocking.)

"I am not reading the Word like I used to." (He's knocking.)

"I'd rather hang out with my *home-boys* rather than be in bible study." (He's knocking.)

"I'd rather go to the club more than church." (He's knocking.)

"Well, I'll go to the club on Saturday, have a few drinks, and then go to church on Sunday." (He's knocking.)

"I cursed this man out because he got on my last nerve." (He's knocking.)

"I'd rather make money than go to the house of God." (He's knocking)

Note:

In this state of mind, we can get so caught up into what we want to do, that sooner or later we will begin to not know what to do. [Even with success in your life.] In this state of mind, you can very well discover that you don't have it together, as much as you thought you did.

"Nice house, nice car, good job, a lot of money; but I can't sleep at night."

When you don't carry out what God is telling you to carry or to do, you will have trouble sleeping.

That was me.

After reading this, I hope that it helps you.

THE ANGER INSIDE

CHAPTER 8

During the course of my "backslidden" and "fallen" status, I suffered several losses. Not just spiritual losses, but natural losses, esteem losses, financial losses, identity losses, and a loss of hope. My cares became careless. After trying so hard to get back on track, I began to believe that nothing good would ever happen to me. I began to believe that I had messed up so bad that the earth around me did not exist. I felt as though I was a *dead man* walking. To behold the doors of opportunity opening or being presented to me was a dream. For some say, "Nothing comes to a sleeper but a dream." I'd say, "Call me a sleepwalker, because I was awake." The doors were closed.

Applying for job after job, walking in the summer's scorching heat, and the winter's freezing cold. I did all of this in one dress suit for several years. Hoping to hear the words, "You Are Hired", I began to think would never happen. I can remember when I totally gave up on trying anything else... and giving in to a life of corruption and sin. Being that I was a preacher at such an early age (13-14 years old), some who may have known me before my fall, would not believe it if I told it.

It was at a time in the winter. Ice and snow were on the ground, but businesses were still open. I walked thirty miles with holes in my shoes and wearing that one dress suit that I previously mentioned. Three prospective places of employment I went to on that day. The first two turned me down. As a result, I tried applying for employment at a fast food restaurant, knowing that I could not return to my normal field and profession. I just knew that McDonald's would hire me. I went in, and the manager told me NO, despite the huge "Now Hiring" sign that was in the window.

Walking back home, I stepped into a big puddle of slushy ice and cold water. My feet were so cold, that I thought they were going to break. I was kicking up water and ice with each step that I took. Once I made it to my mother's house, I did not realize just how angry I was. I was too cold to think. After I warmed up, crying aloud, I said: *"I will never try again!!! The streets is my home. Forget life, I'm gonna try to get it like the hustlers."*

This was some kind of statement coming from a man that was taught the ways of the Lord, Huh? Well, that wasn't so bad...Trust me. It was worse!!!

I suppose you want to know more about how I got to this point...Don't worry. I <u>won't</u> tell it all.

Let me tell you how the flow of anger worked in my life. At night I was depressed. In the day time, I was angry. These two were the only emotional swings that were working on me. Oh! The enemy had a field day with me. Through all of my anger and depression, I never took it out on anyone that was around me. I was well aware of why I was in the shape that I was in. I just couldn't see my way out. Instead of coming back to Jesus: Alcohol, liquor, drugs, and cigarettes became my way out. (It's amazing how when you're broke and have no money, as to how the devil makes it possible to get *treated* to a "substance" that you would typically have to pay for. For example: Getting into places like clubs, without paying a dime.)

Anger within changed my perception and outlook on life. I figured, shucks, "*I can party, hang out, smoke, drink, go to clubs, and don't have to worry about money. This is my way out.*" I decided that I would "dump all of my problems in the ashtray."

I knew better than that, but I did it anyway. Staying "high" all day-every day, was my goal and it was achieved. Not being able to achieve anything else, I found something that "in my eyes" was achievable. "*Get high and forget about everything else.*" This became my drive, my motto, and ultimately, my problem.

It was said to me, "Don't tell your testimony to everybody, because some folk will hold it against you. It will hurt your credibility as a preacher, and the world does not forgive."

Well, the way I see it, if God can deliver me, He can also deliver someone else.

Do me a favor.....After you finish reading this book, give it to somebody else that might be in a similar situation. It just might help.

Some of the things that I went through were because of the bad choices that I made, and being out of the will of God. Other things that I went through, I had no control over. They just happened. Either way, I was yet still angry and did not look for any other ways or methods to escape the trap that the devil had me in. I had totally given up!!

Going to sleep at night being depressed, brought forth so many tears. Then all of a sudden, there were no more tears. I spent about three months searching for those tears. (Truthfully.) This is not some exaggeration to hype you up. It was clear to me that I was no longer depressed. And NO, I was not delivered yet. Something else had taken its place. I was unaware of what was happening to me until later. Continuing my normal cycle of anger funded addictions. Listening to hard core gangster music, I laid down to go to sleep at night, and <u>wrath</u>, was in my heart. Anger within me had taken full control. Being angry was the way I wanted to be.

What are you saying? Let me explain this in a very easy and simple way. Especially for those of you who don't know why some folks are always *mean as a bull*, with no real cause.

Getting angry is different from being angry. When you get angry, there is a cause. Typically, people get angry when something does not "go their way." Anger becomes the effect. This is where I was in between *shifts* in my life. Being angry is a description of what you have become, as in a personality.

Some would say, "I cannot see *this* being you. You did not look angry." My point exactly. A person who has not developed a personality of anger will show their anger as a result of some adverse event. Somewhat like cause-and-effect.

A person who has developed a personality of anger wants to be left alone and isolates themselves from anything that would make him or her happy.

At this point, I am sure that some of you understand. For those of you who do not, let me explain a bit more.

I had developed a personality of anger. This did not shut down any of my emotional responses. <u>For example</u>:

1. When something was funny, I laughed. Did it make me happy? NO.
2. When something was attractive, I looked at it. Did it make me happy? NO
3) Mingling with others, clowning around with home-boys, and even the smoke party. Did it make me happy? NO

Despite being out and about, it was what was on the inside of me that controlled me, anger. Angry is the way that I wanted to be. I wanted to be left alone.

What do you mean by "left alone?" Well, if you called me, we would talk. If you wanted me to go somewhere, my answer would be "let's go". It was not the outer parts of me that did not want to be bothered, but the inner part of me insisting that I be left alone. [*The anger that I had become.*] I needed an <u>inner healing</u>.

<u>Note</u>:

Whenever an <u>inner healing</u> is needed, there is nothing that anyone else can physically do to help. The only thing that you can do for that person is FAST and PRAY.

Yes, that's one of "*them*" kinds. (Matthew 17:21)

I could go on about what was going on, on the inside of me. But, I believe that by now you get the picture.

Being angry, I found myself doing more and more things in secret. Things that only I, myself would want to know about. I was in my own circle. No one came in except for me. I had closed the doors to my heart, and would not open them for anyone. Knocking......Yes, even in the midst of the state of mind that I was in. Jesus was on the other side of the door; knocking and calling my name. At times it was so loud that I would get afraid. Yet, I still did not open the door because I did not want to hear what He had to say.

When someone would ask me, *"How are you doing?"* it would turn and become the fuel that kindled my anger. With a negative response, I would answer. Anger was yet becoming a part of me. When they would again ask, *"how are you?"* my answer would be, *"I'm good."* Meaning, in my state, which was not good, I had become adjusted to 1) anger being good, 2) being good with anger, and 3) being *"good"* angry. I had changed with the changes that took place in my life. (This is the way I must be. Therefore, I'm *good* with that.)

I'm sure that you would like to know more in detail as to how I fell into such a slum… (Don't worry. I <u>won't</u> tell it all.)

<u>Note</u>:

For those who have developed a personality of anger, it's important to know that each individual reacts differently, speaks differently, and thinks differently. So, don't look for everyone in this condition to carry on in the same way or manner.

TIME CLOCKED OUT

CHAPTER 9

Ecclesiastes 3:1-8 says,

To everything there is a season, and a time to every purpose under the heaven:

A time to be born, and a time to die; a time to plant, and a time to pluck up that which is planted;

A time to kill, and a time to heal; a time to break down, and a time to build up;

A time to weep, and a time to laugh; a time to mourn, and a time to dance;

A time to cast away stones, and a time to gather stones together; a time to embrace, and a time to refrain from embracing;

A time to get and a time to lose; a time to keep, and a time to cast away;

A time to rend, and a time to sew; a time to keep silence, and a time to speak;

A time to love, and a time to hate; a time of war, and a time of peace;

Now, look at Ecclesiastes 3:11. It reads:

He hath made everything beautiful in its time: also he hath set the world in their heart, so that no man finds out the work that God maketh from the beginning to the end.

For me, time did not matter anymore. In fact, I no longer believed in time, and did not care what *time* it was. I felt like time would never change. Therefore, change would never come. Positive moments that I could see with my physical eye, such as watching others graduate from college, or watching others receive sports scholarships, watching others receive any awards, recognition, any form of success, so on and so forth.......I never envied, but applauded. I looked at it as a fairy tale that would never happen to me.

Life for me, growing up, wasn't easy. Becoming an adult can be difficult, as I experienced this first hand. I am sure that others can relate.

After reading the opening paragraph of this chapter, I am sure that you understand what I mean by: "Time Clocked Out". A lot of time in my life was spent, working hard to succeed in many areas of my life in which I knew that I had the talents and gifts necessary to be successful. I knew that God had given me all that I was able to do. I would try everything that I could, just to get things going my way. Not weekly, but *all day – every day*. Now, let's not forget that we are looking at this time, as time being separated from God. I did not want to serve God, preach the gospel, or use what He had blessed me with for Him. All that I wanted was SUCCESS and a better life down here on earth.

Some would say, "It takes time…Rome wasn't built in a day…I can't believe that you would just give up like this…You're still young." Now, understand something, such statements are not choice words for someone that has experienced a lifetime of pain and sorrows. The Bible says, "*He that wins souls is wise.*" No matter how old you are, these types of statements will not help anyone that is in a <u>Time Cocked Out</u> state of mind.

The best thing to do, when trying to reach someone in a <u>Time Clocked Out</u> state of mind, is listen to them. At this point in time, you should talk, if you can get them to talk, without making suggestions. Don't have a hero type of "delivery". Place yourself in their shoes, thus making them feel comfortable. Why do I say this? Well, your life might be better than theirs. You can't counsel anyone, like this, based upon your success. You don't know why they are going through. Read the book of Job paying close attention to what is said to him by his own friends, in the midst of his afflictions. You will see.

Time spent striving today for a better tomorrow, only to wake up to a systematic cycle of failure, became a minute-to-minute regret of existence. Habits were easy to create because engaging in the time that I did not want to waste, wasted me. Replacing my efforts with harmful habits, to me, was better than redeeming any time that was lost.

<u>Time</u>, to me, had become my enemy.

So, I defeated my enemy (Time), by letting <u>time</u> pass me by. Staying *high* from the time I'd wake up, until the <u>time</u> I'd go to sleep. IF I woke up after sleeping, I'd start all over and do it again. Time was dead to me. So, I could no longer feel the pain of spending <u>time</u>, or even losing <u>time</u>. (At no cost.)

The whole <u>time</u>, keeping it all to myself, I did not want my loved ones to know of my condition. Being that I had been raised in church and had been taught the *right* way, I did not want them hurt. I did not want them trying to talk me out of my condition. I felt set, because, to me <u>time</u> had set.

"What a mind frame the devil had me in."

I did not look for anything else in <u>time</u> to come, even with prophecy on my life. Everything in <u>time</u>, to me, only offered poverty and pain. (I had never been a selfish person, but this is how I lived.)

In scripture, we hear Job's friends saying, "*Oh, you did not have any patience.*" Well, patience had nothing to do with it.

MAKING CHOICES

CHAPTER 10

There are many choices to make naturally, but only two choices to make spiritually.

Spiritually

Joshua 24:15 says,

And if it seem evil unto you to serve the Lord, <u>choose</u> you this day whom ye will serve; whether the gods which your fathers served that were on the other side of the flood, or the gods of the Amorites, in whose land ye dwell; but as for me and my house, we will serve the Lord.

Spiritually, of course, we have the <u>choice</u> to either serve God or sin.

Naturally

In this world, many opportunities to make <u>choices</u> are laid before us. Each choice has either a good or bad consequence or result. Some people are better at making choices than others. Make a good <u>choice</u>, get good results. Make a bad <u>choice</u>, get bad results. (Basic wholesome teaching, would you say?)

On the contrary, what about making good <u>choices</u> and getting bad results?

Now, this will not make any sense to an individual that has not been through anything like this. Some who haven't experienced this may not agree that this can indeed happen. If this is you, please give this book to someone else that is in a similar situation or condition, or maybe to someone that is suffering from a case of depression. This may be the DELIVERANCE they need that you could not give them.

I've made a few bad <u>choices</u>, which led to a few bad results. But, I've also made a lot of good <u>choices</u> that led to a long string of bad results. (No need for detail.) This is called: "Can't grab life by the horns."

<u>Note</u>:

A person in this state does not want anybody "licking" their wounds; telling them that "it's gonna be okay". At this point, encouraging words are of no effect. Believe it or not, in this state, an encouraging word is like fuel igniting a fire. It's best to back off and pray for that person, if you <u>won't</u> or <u>can't</u> do anything to help.

"But, how can you assume that it's like this with everyone in this state of mind?"

First of all, it's not an assumption… Go outside and try to encourage somebody who has been spinning around in circles without control of the "bull of life" that they have been riding on. Tell somebody, that's given it their best shot for years, and all that they ever tasted was a bitter cup of failure, that "it's gonna be okay". You might not like what happens next.

He that wins souls is wise.

In times like this, it should be understood that this would not be the ideal moment in which to share encouraging words of the sort. It's a moment to pray without telling that person that you are praying for them. They don't have to hear that from you. If you want to help, figure out something that you can <u>do</u> to help, not <u>say</u> to help. Talking at this moment is hurting more than helping, although you mean well. Some may not show it in front of you, but will go home just that much more depressed when the words given to them are not exact and precise for the situation.

Experience tells you this: A person who has made good choices, and has only gotten bad results, begins to feel as though there are no other options, after so long.

So now I ask; is this how you feel?

For me, the answer was Yes. This was me and a whole lot of other people that I know, don't know, and will surely get to know.

At this point, having a mindset that: "There are no other options", our *will* is now held captive without <u>choice</u>. This is a very bad condition to be in. I was here. That's why I can share this with you.

You might ask, "What do you mean: Our will held captive without choice?"

Well, have you ever asked someone, "Why did you do that?" and the answer was: "I didn't have a choice."?

This is what I mean… The will *to do* is confined because the willingness *to do* did not experience the freedom of *getting done*.

There are some people that would say, "Everyone has an opportunity in life. It's what you do with it." True, but not always true. What do you tell a high school graduate that missed an opportunity to go to college because they did not have the money to pay for it; neither were they approved for financial aid? What do you say to those applying for grants and seeking assistance, yet none of their requests were granted and they did not receive the help that they applied for? Even worse, what do you tell a *great* high school athlete, full of potential, that he or she has lost their opportunity to be discovered by a talent scout? After all, they hoped to be scouted, as this would be their opportunity to get a higher education by scholarship. Not only would this be hard for that *great* athlete to accept, but when looking at their team, they see that the coach is choosing players based upon popularity, what clothes they wear, and the shoes that they put on. What happens when the player with holes in his shoes is a better player than the player that has on a brand new pair of Jordan's?

I'm sure you're thinking that I'm making this up as an example, but these examples are true and actually took place. (These are just a few examples.)

People with a mindset as such: "I have no other option." run in the same circle. It would blow some of you away just to hear about some of the situations that others have had to go through in this state of mind.

(One of the best witnesses to reach out is one who has been through the same thing as the person that they are trying to reach out to. After all, he will know what to say.)

The options in <u>making choices</u> are now looked upon as a privilege of <u>making choices</u> when it comes to <u>choosing</u>. This is a privilege that a person in this condition doesn't feel that they have.

How so?

It's very simple. Go, take someone in this troubled condition and buy them a brand new suit. Tell them to pick whatever they want. Observe their actions and their verbal response. (This is the best one...) Go and take someone in this troubled condition, out to eat. Give them a menu. Observe their actions and their verbal response. The response that you get from a person in this particularly troubled condition will not be the same as someone who just doesn't have the money, is in need of clothes, or is hungry.

<u>Note</u>:

This condition is not developed as a result of being without money or material possessions. It has nothing to do with it. So, what you are observing is *their* position in making choices.

As I said before, this will not make sense to someone who hasn't experienced this type of depression...However; this information could very well serve as a useful tool when trying to reach people that are in this mindset.

You can always tell when someone hasn't been through whatever it is that you are going through, just by the way that they advise or try to advise you. This was me and so many others that I know, don't know, and will surely get to know.

CORRECTED
CONVICTED
ACCEPTED

CHAPTER 11

I could go on and on, testifying about my conditions, from the minors to the majors. Each state, here written of, all leads to a physical destruction such as suicide, beginning with a spiritual suicide.

We know that Satan comes to kill, steal, and destroy. One of the main tools that the devil uses is deception. He's the father of lies and if he can get us to believe his lies, he can get us to live in error.

If you notice, each one of the conditions that I have written about had something to do with a feeling…a thought, beginning in the mind; working through the body. From the beginning of time, the devil has always aimed his lies at something specific. When Satan lies, his lie is always about us. A tactic of the enemy, designed to make us error.

Look again at Genesis 3:4-5.

And the serpent (the devil) said unto the woman, ye shall not surely die:

For God doth know that in the day ye eat thereof, then your eyes shall be opened, and ye shall be as gods. *Knowing good and evil.*

Satan, just as he does now, aimed his lie. God told Adam and Eve not to eat of this tree. The devil told them they would be as *gods*, if they did. He lied to them about them. So, they walked in error because they believed his lie.

How many people do you know that are living their lives, defeated by depression, anger, regret, etc…all because they believed the lie that the devil told them about themselves. When Satan gets a crack, he opens the door wide. Every Single Time.

What are the cracks?

1. Failure is a crack.

   The devil opens the door, comes right in, and lies to us. *"You know you're never gonna make it. It's never gonna work out for you."*

2.   <u>Anger</u> is a crack.

The devil likes this door because he can control us more when he comes in and tells us to do something. His lie here makes you feel safe doing what you do.

3.   <u>Regret</u> is a crack.

The devil comes in this door to lie about it being "all your fault".

4.   <u>Worry</u> is a crack.

The devil comes in this door to lie about provisions that <u>do not</u> belong to you.

5.   <u>Fear</u> is a crack.

The devil comes in this door to lie about something bad happening, when doing something good.

6)   <u>Weariness</u> is a crack.

In this crack, the devil lies about your good efforts, making you feel like they were all for nothing.

Satan will never stop taking his opportunities. His job is to lie and deceive. This is not his talent. He first has to get in, thus giving him an inside opportunity to lie to you. Satan uses his talents to get in.

Go back to Genesis 3:1:

Now the <u>serpent</u> was more <u>subtle</u> than <u>any beast of the field which the Lord God had made</u>. And he said unto the woman, yea hath God said, ye shall not eat of every tree of the garden.?

This suggests that the serpent was not the devil himself, but the devil spoke through the serpent. Instead of using any other beast that God created, the devil used the serpent which was, at that time, the most beautiful, clever creature during its non-cursed state. The devil came in clever, which was by talent, then began deceiving. The question here, asked of Eve, was deceitful. For it was designed to suggest that God was unfair to restrict them from eating of this tree. Satan waits for an opportunity, he never waits to lie. Anyone can be deceived at any time. All that Satan needs is an opening. Satan can use anyone and anything to deceive God's people. He always comes in with his talents.

Jesus spoke of the way that Satan seeks to get in.

Matthew 24:23-24

Then if any man shall say unto you, lo, here is Christ, or there, believe them not.

For there shall arise false christs, and false prophets, and shall shew great signs and wonders; insomuch that, if it were possible, they shall deceive the very elect.

This suggests that instead of using a serpent, Satan will use man. Man will be used to do signs and wonders; to come in and deceive the very elect of God's people.

These are the signs to look for these last days. As it has always been from the beginning of time, Satan is doing his job as usual.

All deception is of the devil, even if we deceive ourselves.

James 1:26 says,

If any man among you seem to be religious, and bridleth not his tongue, but deceiveth his own heart; this man's religion is vain.

Satan's plan is to cause us to walk and live in error. This has always been the plan, and will always be his plan. If he can succeed in this, he can take our lives, both here and in eternity.

We see in Revelation 20, the same mission. Even after the thousand years, Satan is loosed and goes right back to what he does best; deceiving the people. Over and over again. The belief system is hard to break, and the devil knows this. This is why he does the best he can do to bring deception amongst us.

There is a statement that people use when trying to encourage a person. Do you remember what it is?.......It goes like this, "Oh. Don't be so hard on yourself." Typically, the response would be, "Well, it's true.".....

Many instances of failure, listening to the devil speak during times of sorrow, and other emotional swings, all lead to that particular person believing negative things about *themselves*. Someone on the other side would usually say, "This person just wants somebody to show them some sympathy." In actuality, this is not the case. Simply put: NOT SO!

This really is what is believed of this person and the last thing that they probably want is sympathy. In fact, sympathy would build more anger right in the center of things that are going on and things to come.

PRAYER IS THE KEY.

LESS THAN A MAN

CHAPTER 12

A working man wants to do nothing more than work and provide for his family, take care of the house, etc. Independence is his position. For the record, there are a lot of things that can happen that could strip a man of his integrity, rob his identity, and break the back of his confidence.

What are some of these things? (Talking to the Real Men!)

1) A bad marriage.
2) Inability to work due to an unfavorable background. (*Innocent or guilty, he yet tries.*)
3) Being taken advantage of.
4) Becoming a father, and being placed on child support; just for the sake of its benefits, not for the interest of the child.
5) Being a father that is under the hand of an evil "baby-mother". (*This is fact ladies. Don't get mad at me.*)

Note:

For those of you who are divorced and have children, it's important to treat the children with fairness. Women, if you know that your children's father loves them, don't try to use the children to control him. This will cause greater problems, not to mention: This Is Wrong!!!

A real life disaster! The relationship between the father and his children is crippled when women use the children to control the father. Ultimately, the children suffer as a result. We hear the father's plea, "I've done everything that I could possibly do. Recovery will never happen, my hands are bound, and my feet are tied up!"

What else is a man supposed to do?

Oh! ..... Joseph Paul Brown is Mad Now!!!!

This is one of the main ways that the devil wants to take our manhood from us. Ways to strip a man of his integrity, rob his identity, and break the back of his confidence.

What else is a man supposed to do?

"Why am I asking this when I should know the answer?"

I see now. Maybe it's because I am less than a man. What am I? I don't know yet. But a man, the way my life if going seems farfetched from what the image of a man should be.

<u>Note</u>:

Feeling "less than a man" is an emotional disorder, which suggests that he once knew what it felt like to be a man via performance and by carrying the things that men carry responsibly.

Paul said in <u>1 Corinthians 13:11</u>:

When I was a child, I spoke as a child, I understood as a child, I thought as a child: but when I became a <u>man</u>, I put away childish things.

So, is it possible to no longer *think as a man?* Let me answer that for you. The answer is Yes. Ironically, Satan has always, in some way, come up with a plan to alter this. He seeks to take our manhood. (Homosexuality is not the only way.)

Go back to Genesis 3 again. It reads:

For God doth know that in the day ye eat thereof, then your eyes shall be opened, <u>and ye shall be as</u> gods. Knowing good and evil.

Look at the lie that Satan speaks in this passage of scripture. The aim here, in this attempt was to take their manhood. Not by making them feel like they were "less than a man", but by making them feel like they were "more than a man". But, it all works the same and comes from the same force. Satan, lying as he always does, wanted to change something from its original design by polluting, contaminating, and perverting God's creation.

One ounce of weakness in a man; the devil magnifies it in effort to make you feel like you are <u>less than a man</u>.

One ounce of strength; the devil magnifies it in effort to make you feel like you are <u>more than a man</u>.

Both of these are deadly forces that attack the character of a true man; bringing death to his spirit and harm to his body. A man at work in full capacity is operating in the dominion and power that God gave him from the very beginning. He is able to rest and be at peace after accomplishing his mission, perhaps after many hours of labor.

We saw what happens at the hand of excessive lust for more power, above the natural strengths and abilities that are given. Now, let's look more at what happens below the strength and abilities that God gives him.

A man who has functioned in his God given position, experiences the refreshing sensation of walking in his authority. Taking care of business, successfully handling what is entrusted to him. When this is no longer happening, the blessing thereof, is now looked upon as a privilege in his eye. A privilege he no longer has. The dominion here, given a man, to be in control of stewarding and governing that which is created… (substance) puts him, man, on top of things. This is the *proper* order and position that God ordained from the very beginning of time.

GOD ABOVE MAN-MAN ABOVE CREATION.

If man moves below this order, it would put him below creation. Doing such would put creation above man, rather than God. As a result, God is no longer in "control" over man; therefore man is out of control.

In this state of mind, people react differently. Some handle feeling "less than a man" by committing crimes, stealing, robbing, selling drugs, etc…Ask them why they did it and the answer will be, "I couldn't get a job; I have to survive; My children have to eat." At this point, it is obvious that such is not the proper arrangement of manhood. It could be said that "I lost my control of things when I lost my job. Now things control me. The idea of seeing others drive nice cars controls me to do what it is that I do, to drive nice cars too." When a man has reached this point or state of mind, he needs to be returned to his manhood. Where this man should be in control of money, the money now controls him. Here is where a man would do just about anything, below the original design that God had intended for him, all to get whatever it is that he thinks he needs to get.

Observe Creation.

God created sex for husband and wife, but pornography and X-Rated films promote sex outside of marriage. What is there to gain out of all of this production of perversion? We know that the production team is paid, as well as the willing parties or actors. Where is man? At this point, is he at the top of the order? Is he at the bottom of the order? Is he not in the order at all?

Note:

We are controlled by whatever it is that makes us <u>feel</u> like we are less than what God has made us to be. We are controlled by whatever it is that makes us <u>feel</u> like we are more than what God has created us to be. Both of these lead to error, and Satan knows it.

When my dad says. "Son, be a man.", in the condition of <u>feeling</u> less than a man, it almost makes you feel like a discouraged victim under a load of materialistic burdens that you have not the strength, power, nor control to lift. Though dad spoke well, the burden got heavier.

The push and motivation to be a man, from a father to his teenage son, is taken as a progressive statement from the father to the son, pushing him to step up to the plate. Hearing such when in the state of feeling "less than a man", is less likely profitable and fully accepted because the son is stripped of all possible dignity that could help him develop into a man. Therefore, the response is different all together.

You never know what makes a man, which <u>feels</u> "less than a man", tick. At least not until you see what it is that he does, and why he does it. You don't have to be a doctor to figure that out. The error here is found when people try to "build" a man who <u>feels</u> "less than a man". It does not work. The correct way and manner in which to help, is to *rebuild* the man that <u>feels</u> "less than a man". Being that he once felt like a man, he needs to be rebuilt and not built. At this point, you will see results.

"I'm less than a man because I know what a real man can do. Real men make good decisions. Real men take care of business. Real men work hard. Real men have wives. Real men walk tall. Real men make it happen!!! Real men serve God, and creation serves real men!!!. (The proper order.)

All of this stuff that I can't do. I have no way of getting it done. I'm pressed in with perplexity. So, what am I to do?

I do the things that real men don't do.....

Why?

Because I <u>feel</u> less than a man.

Why do I feel this way?

Because Satan lied to me and I believed it!!!

OVERCOMING
IN VICTORY

CHAPTER 13

After being trapped by bitter walls of failure and living a life as low as I went, victory was not necessarily in eyesight. It was not until I returned to the *voice* that had been calling me in the midst of the state that I was in. This same voice, speaking to my heart, was also speaking through the preached word of God; across the pulpit, confirming everything spoken.

In my life, getting victory was more of an intense fight, than losing the victory that I had already walked in….hum…interesting. Whenever the devil is losing and eventually loses a soul that he thought he had, he puts up a fight and doesn't give in easy. Before I could overcome, I first had to get the victory, which is in Christ Jesus.

Where faith once worked, I had to learn how to work faith all over again. As I began to come back to the Lord, I had to train all over again. Reading the word daily, listening with not only my ears, but also with my heart. Receiving the word by faith; praying and wrestling with God at night. It wasn't easy.

The spirit within me, that was broken, had to be restored. The road and journey ahead, was even more difficult when trying to come back to the Lord. Getting the victory, I had to face many obstacles, as I think and reflect back upon that time. It was during this time that I realized that "overcoming" was what I would have to do.

For instance: Facing others who had known me in the beginning of my ministry, who knew of my fallen state and downfall, even facing those who would encourage me to come back to God in love, was yet still difficult. But, this was all a part of Satan's forces fighting against my DELIVERANCE.

Yet, and still, out of all of my encounters, striving to get back in the *fold*, to be restored, my strength was coming from God. Those who went before God for me, those who never said a word to me, but only prayed or spoke when God said "speak"; it was even through them that God sent strength. I could always feel the Lord pushing me at this point. At this point I felt like Jonah coming out of the belly of a fish with seaweed all over him.

This was the "dropping" point for me. The point where I knew what I looked like and I knew that others could see me as well. Despite it all, it didn't matter to me because all <u>feelings</u> were beginning to be overcome.

God spoke to me of a *destiny* that I would have to reach! After so many failures in my life, I could not see failure ahead. Not knowing how to get there, just walking towards it with nothing in my hands; No money, no job, wearing hand-me-down clothes that barely fit. I even had some that had faded over time.

Overcoming? Yes. The fact of being seen in a mess and as a mess, no longer bothered me because I could not feel the sting of what the enemy was using to make me turn around. The devil used everything that he could, just to get me off the track to Overcoming in Victory. I don't really know how everything suddenly began to change, but I do know that my mind was changed. In my mind, I could think of nothing more than where I was going, though unsure as to where it was, or how to get there. (Especially being broke and all.) My mind had taken on this *pure* outlook of the future that would minister to people, build, and rebuild lives. A *pure* outlook, yet and while my life was still broken. It is interesting how God works. My life is a living testimony, of how God can take nothing and make something. How God can take a "nobody" and make him somebody.

I began to ask God to get the glory out of my life, even with the way that my life was. I don't know how He could get any glory out of my life at all, except He lifts me out of my "self" first. So, I began to ask God to lift me out of my "self" and get the glory out of my life. The "self" that had messed up everything, had to be lifted out first in order for God to come in and fix it. As a result, He would get the glory out of it all.

For how could man, all of a sudden, go from lack to abundance? From deprivation to opportunity? From poverty to prosperity? From smelling bad to smelling good? From vision to provision? Even from a jacked up state, such as what's been described, except it all come from God?

Does God make "ways" out of "no ways"?

My life speaks today. Yes! He does. Even when I said, "He doesn't for me", He proved me wrong.

I've been CORRECTED.

I am CONVICTED.

It is ACCEPTED.

As a young teen, preaching without any experience from the world of sin and fleshly fulfilments. Beginning at the age of thirteen, all the way to the age of nineteen, I could only preach with *conviction*; no real life experiences of bondage or control of dark forces.

So, the message of "Victory in the Cross", according to Colossians, was only a message of conviction. Preached, believed, and received as the word was going forth. That settled it. I had no *dirt* that needed to be washed away by the Blood of Jesus, but I knew that it was real and could be done. Therefore, I preached it as so.

However, entering into the fallen state, coming out with the victory, and overcoming the world; all brought forth the experience of TRUE redemption at the CROSS. I now find these instances and experiences more useful in ministry.

Where the devil says, "How you gonna preach with such a bad background?"

God says, "You have experienced me. So, you have more than just a message, you have a story to tell."

Yes. I used to preach with conviction. Now I can preach with experience and conviction. Where I was saved as a young baby boy, I was *just* saved. But, when I came back to the Lord, and experienced salvation in a way that I had not experienced it before. I was saved from the bondage of sin and shame, the operations of the flesh; which had me bound to a body of destruction. There is victory in the cross that breaks the power of any dominating force. There is victory in the cross that breaks the curse that sin brings. There is victory in the cross that defeats the enemies of it. There is victory in the cross, in which all opposing forces, sickness, and disease must fall behind.

Where sin had me contaminated and dirty, I have now been washed and cleansed by the blood of Jesus, in which all who sin must experience, in order to be made whole.

I never had dirty thoughts as a young boy, being saved so early. In my fallen state, I picked up dirty thoughts. The blood of Jesus washed my thoughts.

I was transformed by the renewing of my mind.

Romans 12:2 says,

Be not conformed to this world, but be ye transformed by the renewing of your mind, that ye may prove what is that good, and acceptable, and perfect will of God.

It was not God's will for me to have a corrupted mind. Satan wants our minds to be corrupt. Since my mind was corrupt, my heart became corrupt. Whatever gets into your mind, gets into your heart. Whatever gets into the heart, comes out of the mouth. This defiled me.

Matthew 15:18-19 reads:

But those things which proceed out of the mouth come forth from the heart; and they defile the man.

For out of the heart proceed evil thoughts, murders, adulteries, fornications, theft, false witness, blasphemies:

Proverbs 4:23 brings it home for me.

Keep thy heart with all diligence; for out of it are the issues of life.

I allowed what the "eye gate" and the "ear gate" heard and saw, to get into my mind and enter into my heart, which was corrupt. Therefore, I began to live a life of corruptions.

<u>Note</u>:

One cannot guard the heart when looking at and listening to corruptible things… Our strengths can be weakened. This is why we are instructed to guard our hearts.

This is what I did not do. - As a result, I became dirty. Furthermore, as a result, I blessed the Lord!!! I was able to experience the wonder working power that the saints would sing about; "In the blood of the lamb."

No longer do I live in defeat, below the dignity of the man that God has created me to be. No longer am I under the control of worldly powers, found in material things that could be temporarily running my life.

I've got the VICTORY and I am an OVERCOMER.

I am in control of all things through the power of God. I am walking in my rightful place, lined up according to the word of God.

I am CORRECTED.

I am CONVICTED.

It is ACCEPTED.

God is in control of me. The divine order. God created the things of this earth, and he created me as well. He created me as a man, to control these things that are down here on this earth. More so, I refuse to let these things down here on this earth control me, including the *flesh*.

I am CORRECTED.

I am CONVICTED.

It is ACCEPTED.

Drugs can't control me, because I refuse to be drugged!

People can't control me, because I refuse to be controlled by mere humans that want to mislead me.

Now that I am an overcomer; Now that I am walking in victory; I refuse to be defeated again.

[Because] The Spirit that controls me is the Spirit that leads me.

Father God, I thank you for this opportunity to share my story and to deliver a message at the same time. I thank you for the deliverance that has taken place in my life. A deliverance that only you could have done.

I pray now father, that the readers of this book be eternally blessed, some saved, some delivered, and some set free, by your mighty power.

Bring forth inner healing in the lives of your people. Restore, revive, and renew. Let your glory be revealed to us and in us. Do it for us Jesus, according to your word. For you would that no man should perish.

Be glorified and highly exalted for all men to see and receive, and I will be careful to give your name the praise and the glory, both now and forever; It's in Jesus' name I pray.

AMEN